COPING WITH DEATH
Fourth Edition

Also by Leslie Scrase:

**new fourth edition**

# COPING WITH DEATH

a book for the bereaved &
those who try to help them

## Leslie Scrase

UNITED WRITERS
Cornwall

UNITED WRITERS PUBLICATIONS LTD
Ailsa, Castle Gate, Penzance, Cornwall.

British Library Cataloguing in Publication Data:
A catalogue record for this book is
available from the British Library.

ISBN 9781852002053

*First published in 1990
Second Edition 1996
Third Edition 2002
New Fourth Edition 2021*

Printed in Great Britain by
United Writers Publications Ltd
Cornwall.

To the memory of Karuna Anne, my daughter,
and Alison, my granddaughter.

# The Author

The author conducted his first ceremony, a Sunday service in a small chapel in North Devon, when he was 17 years old. When this edition comes out, he will have been conducting ceremonies of one kind or another for 70 years. He became a minister of religion, serving in various parts of this country and in South India over a period of about 20 years.

Loss of religious faith took him to the British Humanist Association and the conduct of Humanist ceremonies from the late 1970s until now. He sees himself as no more than a voice, attempting to enable people to achieve the kind of ceremony they desire. Inevitably this involves a good deal of flexibility and openness.

For many years he conducted over a hundred ceremonies a year and this had risen to over 150 a year, which suggests that there is a need for celebrants to take this kind of approach. Now past his 90th birthday, he is almost retired.

Twice married, he and Wendy share six children and a host of grandchildren scattered through the south of England, Denmark and (probably) Norway.

# Contents

# Preface

When I was still a minister of religion, one of my colleagues was the Revd. Clement Pugsley. A genuine pastor, he had written a small book called *In Sorrows Lone Hour*. It was that book which led me, many years ago, to try to provide a book for people with no religious faith.

The kindness of a Finnish friend and publisher, Markku Vartiainen, got the first edition of my *Coping with Death* off the ground. It went through three editions and several thousand copies but parts of it had become pretty dated. The world has changed since I first began conducting secular ceremonies, well over forty years ago, before there were any training schemes for secular celebrants.

There *were* secular celebrants around serving members of different secular societies but few, if any, of them, offered their services to the general public. I must have been one of the very first to do so. Nowadays funeral directors are faced with an embarrassment of riches with hosts of celebrants of all shades of opinion available.

As my own life draws to its close, with something over 6,000 funerals behind me, I have decided to gather together some of my own writings in the hope that they may prove to be of comfort and help to people facing the death of those they love.

I conducted my first ceremony, a Sunday service in a small Methodist chapel in North Devon, when I was 17 years old and I have warm memories of the kindness and hospitality of the people I served back then. Generous hospitality was a mark of Methodists in those far off days – perhaps it still is.

9

After serving for nearly twenty years as a minister of religion in different parts of this country and in South India and (briefly) in the USA, I found that I no longer believed the things that had made me a minister.

My changed attitude to religion can be found in three books:

*An Unbeliever's Guide to the Bible*
*The Four Gospels through an Outside Window*
*Belief, Unbelief, Ethics and Life*

All of these were published by United Writers Publications and are still available – and also to be found in some libraries. I owe an immense debt of gratitude to Malcolm Sheppard of United Writers who also published the third edition of *Coping with Death*.

Finally, I owe a huge debt to my second wife Wendy who has put up with me for over 45 years and given me the freedom to pursue my own interests and concerns.

In the course of a lifetime, I have seen great poverty and hardship. I have seen disease at its most destructive – and of course, we have all now been confronted by the ravages of Covid-19. I have spent a good deal of time with those who were dying and with those who have been bereaved. And, of course, I have lost loved ones of my own. You can't live for ninety plus years without doing so.

Death and bereavement are part of our universal experience. But there is something very special about being allowed to share in the intimate moments of other people's grief. At its best, such sharing can be mutually strengthening. But with, or without, the support of others, again and again in my lifetime I have seen the human spirit rise from the depths and triumph over the worst that life can bring. If this book is of the slightest help in achieving that kind of triumph, it will have achieved its purpose.

*Leslie Scrase*

# Part One

# *Practical*
## *and*
# *Philosophical*

# I

# Some Practicalities

When a loved one dies we are often distracted beyond words. We don't know what to do.

As long as there was life there were things that we could do even if we were only sitting by someone's bedside. But now that they have gone, even that last ministry of companionship is meaningless and we feel totally lost.

Perhaps the first thing to do is to make yet another 'good cup of tea'. (When my mother-in-law read that she said, "Make mine a gin!") Unless we are one of those very independent people who wish to do everything ourselves and to keep everything in our own hands, the second thing to do is to call the funeral director.

We can safely leave most things in his or her hands. The funeral director knows what has to be done. Some things s/he will do. Others will be left to us – but s/he will tell us what we have to do and how to go about it.

Doing all that has to be done at a time when we are full of grief and pretty exhausted is demanding but it can also be therapeutic. In dealing with the past, we are taking our first tentative steps forward into the future.

# II

# The Funeral Ceremony

With the passing of the centuries beliefs come and go, fashions and styles of mourning change. Customs vary from place to place and many of the customs current when I was a lad have gone completely. Few people now wear black. Neighbours no longer feel the need to close their curtains. Men no longer raise their hats when a hearse passes – they no longer wear hats!

And coffins have changed too. Many people try to use coffins that are 'environmentally friendly'. Cardboard is not as friendly as many people imagine. Somerset willow is probably the most friendly source at the moment.

At any funeral there are people holding a variety of different opinions. Within a perfectly ordinary congregation those opinions can vary quite widely from atheistic at one extreme to evangelical religious at the other. It is important to be aware of our differences and sensitive to one another and to try to make space within a ceremony for people of all opinions to find something of support and strength. We all need to feel that we are included and that we have the opportunity to share in what is going on.

Funerals are not the place for evangelicalism of any kind. Celebrants are not there to try to persuade us to their own form of belief or unbelief, and any who feel that that is their task should be removed from the funeral director's list.

Death faces us with universal human needs which bind us all together. We need to find suitable ways in which to express our grief. We need to honour those we have loved and to express our love as generously as we can and we need to find the strength to begin our own lives all over again.

Since no two bereavements are the same and no two people are the same, it follows that no two funerals should be the same.

A specimen order of ceremony follows this chapter. In secular ceremonies, the centrepiece will usually be some form of tribute or eulogy. We celebrate the lives our loved ones have lived and perhaps re-examine our own in the light of them, asking whether we are living our own lives the best way we can.

Most funerals nowadays are at a crematorium. The main disciplining factor is the time allowed. If that is not enough, double slots can be booked. It is simple courtesy to those who will come after us to adhere to the time limits laid down. Having said that, those who own and run crematoria should recognise that people do need time to do things decently. My own view is that there should always be 45 minutes between ceremonies (even if that involves a slight reduction in profits!). It allows mourners the time to feel that they are not just on a conveyor belt.

For many families 'the committal' is the worst moment of all. It seems to be the moment of final farewell. Many people feel that it's an essential part of the ceremony. If it is, then it should not be the last element in the ceremony. There needs to be something short and uplifting after the committal.

Other families prefer simply to leave the coffin on view until after they leave the chapel, thus avoiding those stressful moments.

Finally it probably needs to be said that nowadays at a funeral, anything goes. Within the time slot we have, anybody can take part – speaking, singing, playing instruments, even dancing – or just being silent. And increasingly, families are dispensing with any kind of celebrant!

I don't think any of these things matter as long as the funeral celebrates the life of the person who has died and expresses our gratitude for a life we have shared and enjoyed. My own preference is that these things are done quietly, with care, respect and dignity.

# A Specimen order of service ceremony:

**Opening music as coffin enters**

**Opening sentences**

Many will feel that these are unnecessary, but they are one means of settling people down and leading them into the ceremony proper.

**Opening reading**

There are masses to choose from, many on the internet (where they are not always accurate or attributed to the right authors).

**General Introduction**

This is virtually the only place where the celebrant puts his/her own stamp on the ceremony. After visiting the family it should have become clear what some of the family's priorities are and what some of their needs are in terms of comfort and support. The introduction will be the one place where the celebrant really tries to insert something helpful and of lasting value.

**Tribute/Eulogy**

Presented by the celebrant or by a member of the family or a family friend.

**Music or Quiet Time**

Two or three minutes spent quietly can give an opportunity for people to find their own path of peace or, if they are so inclined, to say their prayers.

**Committal**

Religious ceremonies have their own forms of committal, many of them including the famous words 'earth to earth (at a graveside), dust to dust, ashes to ashes.' My own committals usually follow one of the following patterns but there are no rules!

Death is part of the natural order of things.
It belongs to the life of the world.
It is the condition of our existence.
It is but nature's way, there is nothing to fear.
So we commit your loved one to his/her natural end
(earth to earth), dust to dust, ashes to ashes.

or

We commit you
into the cycle of living and dying
(into the darkness and warmth of the earth),
into the freedom of wind and of sunshine,
into the dance of the stars and the planets,
and into the richness and smiles of our memories.

I usually follow the words of committal with some brief, forward-looking sentences aimed at being uplifting.

The ceremony ends with a final reading and final words – the last taking the place of a religious blessing and sending us away as helpfully and kindly as possible (see the final pages of this book).

# III

# Untimely Death

Some deaths are much harder to face than others. When those who die are young, grief may be hell.

We no longer face the fact of our mortality as early in life as we used to do. Back in the 1960s I lived in India for a while. At that time the average expectation of life was just over forty, and two out of three children died before they were five.

When life is that short you take your own mortality for granted. But when the average is up in the seventies, it is very easy to ignore the fact that none of us is guaranteed a tomorrow. After listening to a conversation between my father and one of his great-grandchildren I wrote:

> When you grow up my grandson
> and schooldays are over for you,
> when all of your training is finished
> what do you think you will do?

> > I'm still very small my grandpa
> > like a bud on your favourite rose
> > and whether or not I shall flower
> > is something that nobody knows.

> > Make the most of the bud my grandpa,
> > take pleasure from what you can see.

It's what I am now that matters,
don't bother with what I will be.

You are right my wise young grandson
the bud is the thing to enjoy
for my flower will be blown and over
while you are no more than a boy.

I came to terms with my own mortality as a boy of seventeen. I was on holiday with my parents and my sister and we were walking near Land's End. I had lagged behind and was watching the sea crashing against the foot of the cliffs below.

In those circumstances water can have a dangerous attraction, a sort of drawing power. Perhaps this is what the ancient Greeks meant by the sirens. I have felt it often since – felt it with particular power inside a mountain in Switzerland watching the Trummelbach Falls.

On that day, watching the sea at Land's End, it came to me that (whatever it might mean to anybody else) it would not matter to me if I died there and then. I had had a good life; a complete life as far as it went.

From that moment I have known that *for the person who dies* it doesn't matter whether he/she is seven, seventeen or seventy. What matters is whether life has been good up to that moment.

If we have had a good life, death is meaningless to us. If we have not, death may well be that 'merciful release' so many people talk about.

It is only for other people, the loved ones we leave behind, that our death has meaning.

When I realised these things I knew that my own death would never worry me. I was ready for it whenever it came and I would live my life as fully as I could for as long as it lasted.

A long time ago I visited a teenage girl who was dying. She wasn't worried that she was dying – except for one thing. She was still a virgin and felt that she had missed out. Apart from that, though life had been brief it had been very good. Yet I still find myself thinking about her quite often – and she died over fifty years ago. If a friend's sense of loss continues, how much worse must it be for her family? The death of the young may not be a problem to those who die, but it is terrible for those who survive. And often grief is compounded by the circumstances of the death.

Cot death takes our babies; suicide our students; drug addiction and drink-driving take teens and twenties; crime kills; and 'aids' also attacks and destroys the young.

Although so very different, all these kinds of death pose special problems. However innocent we are, we often feel guilty. And it doesn't matter how reassuring other people are, we can still feel guilty. There is that awful 'if only. . .' hanging over us.

And we also feel that there are people who are pointing the finger of blame. I have had that finger of blame pointed at me and after forty years it still rankles and hurts.

When caring people lose a baby they are often inconsolable. None of us can watch over a child for twenty-four hours a day, but distraught parents constantly punish themselves for not being there at the crucial time. They are not blameworthy but they blame themselves nonetheless – and there are always those who will turn the screw.

All that any of us can do is to show faith in them and to support them with our ongoing love.

When older youngsters die, the responsibility is often clearer and sometimes all too clear. After a murder we blame the murderer. After a car crash we can often blame the folly or irresponsibility of car drivers. Sometimes in our search for relief from grief we damn too fiercely and our anger covers the fact that we do not feel entirely free from guilt ourselves.

It is very human and very understandable, but we should try to remember that the killers have their own burden of guilt to bear. Cursing them or punishing them may be necessary and helpful, but in the end we shall be left with our own grief and we shall have to find our own ways of coming to terms with it. We have lost someone we love. Hatred and bitterness will not bring that person back. It will only sour our own life and destroy it. Even if we cannot forgive, we must come to terms with what has happened and learn to live again.

One of the hardest deaths to face is that of a young suicide. I think particularly of one young student who actually came home to his loving, caring family at Christmastime and committed suicide at home. No family could have been more loving and supportive. Yet now they had to face the utter devastation of his death and all the unanswerable questions it left behind. They are one of the loveliest families it has ever been my privilege to meet yet it happened to them.

Death from 'aids' also poses special problems. Whether the victim is heterosexual or not, families often feel ashamed and want no mention made of the cause of death. It is the Christian obsession with sex and with its own prurient morality which has created this shame and its attendant feelings of guilt. In this, as in so much else, religion is the source of much of humanity's pain instead of being a source of peace and healing.

Death from sexually transmitted diseases is not necessarily shameful at all. I have taken the funerals of many aids victims and have only rarely felt that there was any just cause of shame.

Where the victim is a homosexual or where a lesbian dies young there are often special problems of a kind rarely met in any other sort of death.

Families have often rejected their homosexual or lesbian children. Now that it is too late, they often want to ease their sense of guilt and their grief by making amends and they suddenly become very loving and possessive.

But their child has often become part of a new, gay or lesbian 'family'. Homosexuals and lesbians often form very loving, very supportive communities and these are as possessive and protective as the natal family that now suddenly appears on the scene.

A great deal of sensitivity and understanding is needed on all sides. In my experience, the gay/lesbian communities often show these qualities in a very marked degree.

Those of us who have to conduct the funerals of aids victims often feel that we are walking a tightrope. But it is a tightrope well worth walking. The rewards, if we can bring a measure of help and comfort all round, are enormous. I called this chapter 'Untimely Death' which is a daft heading when you come to think of it. Death is nearly always untimely. Usually it comes too early. But sometimes it comes too late. In that case our mourning often begins long before our loved one dies.

Accident, illness or advanced old age often mean that we see our nearest and dearest losing their faculties and becoming less than they once were. We grieve to see them thus, and we grieve and are angry because we are helpless to do anything for them.

Sometimes there comes a point where they are ready to die. The law still makes it impossible for anyone to help them on their way. We often feel angry with medical staff who feel as helpless as we do – although there are times when that anger is justified. There are times when doctors and nurses work too hard to keep people alive when life has become meaningless.

Joining a voluntary euthanasia society and/or writing a living will while we are still mentally competent may help to counter that particular problem.

But there are also occasions where, if we are honest, we have to admit that we wish our loved ones were dead because they are no longer the people we loved and respected. Hurt, shame, anger, guilt, grief, helplessness all combine to make us miserable and death often proves to be a genuine relief.

There are times when the real meaning of death is that those who survive can turn back to life. Colin Murray Parkes wrote: 'The essential message of a funeral is that in every ending there is a beginning.' That is also the essential message of death.

There is no greater honour we can pay to those whose lives are over than to turn back to life and to live it to the full. This does not imply forgetfulness or negligence or lack of respect. It simply means that we have learned (often from them) that 'life is for living'. They have had their lives. Part of ours still lies ahead.

But turning back to life is not always easy. Long term carers may have become isolated, imprisoned by the needs of the person to whom they have devoted so many years of their life. They may feel that it is very difficult to begin again, to take the first faltering steps back into a world that has moved on.

And if they are alone they may feel all the difficulty that is faced by those who are single or divorced. They are the odd one out, difficult to invite and shunned because it is felt to be awkward to converse with those who have recently faced death. They will need all the friendship and love we can give. That is it really. In this business of coping with death there are no experts and each death is unique. We have to find our own way through, picking up a crumb of help here and seeing a glimmer of light there.

Other people will usually not know how to help us, and if they are helpful it will often be by pure fluke. Except that they could not help at all but for the fact that they have shown their love and care and entered into our grief with that genuine sympathy which is the sharing of someone's experience.

Coping with death is the same as coping with life. It is simply a matter of drawing on the rich resources of our own humanity and taking strength from our own inner being. Beyond that, it is a matter of drawing on the reservoirs of friendship and love which we have built up over the years and with which we are surrounded.

I do not offer religion or mystique of any kind because I do not believe in them. We are just ordinary human beings, part of the natural world, living through nature's most dreadful storm and finding our way through to a peace of mind and spirit which is our own and all the better for that. With that peace comes the possibility of renewal of life – our very own life, to be lived in all its richness until it too comes to its end in death – a death which will be somebody else's problem.

# IV

# Life after Death?

Right through history there have been those who hankered after some sort of life after death and there have been those who did not. Our generation is no exception.

Within my own family, my mother had no interest in the subject and was completely agnostic about it. As far as she was concerned, she didn't know whether there was another life and she didn't care. That was the end of the matter.

My father, on the other hand, has been obsessed with the subject for as long as I can remember. His ideas involve a whole series of contradictions – but all of us are guilty of that from time to time. I suspect that he keeps them in separate watertight compartments and trots out whichever is preeminent at the moment. Sometimes he believes in a kind of afterlife school. We join the school at whatever level our life on earth has entitled us to and work our way up from say Class Three Heaven to Class Two and so on. At other times he believes in some form of human reincarnation. When I wrote this he was ninety-five years of age, so he was in no hurry to put his ideas to the test.

But enough of my family. Let us look a little wider.

In ancient times those who longed for life after death had fairly vague ideas and hopes. But they included using heavy stones to keep the dead down and prevent them from causing malicious harm to the living. They also included filling graves with the sort of possessions which might come in useful in another life: clothes, tools, weapons, wives, horses and servants.

As people tried to develop their thinking two kinds of idea became common: Hindus, Buddhists and others came up with some form of the reincarnation idea – the belief that we don't just live one life, we live a succession of lives. Sometimes this is seen as a progression towards the goal of absorption into the One, the All.

The other idea is more familiar to us in the West. It seems to have been developed first of all by a brotherhood of religious reformers in Palestine. They were known as the Hasidim and became the Pharisees of New Testament times.

It comes as something of a surprise to many people to learn that the Jews of Old Testament times had no real belief in life after death. Their ideas were not so very different from those of the Greeks. Hades or Sheol was the place of the dead. There the ghosts or shades lived on in a fairly meaningless kind of way. The dead Achilles told Odysseus that he would rather be a living slave than a dead prince.

The Hasidim developed the idea that after death there is a resurrection for those who have lived good or godly lives. A new life has been stored up for them with God.

Christians took this idea over and developed it, supporting it with miracles such as the raising of Lazarus from death by Jesus and the resurrection of Jesus himself. Moslems also took the idea over (initially from the Jews) and developed their own rather sensual idea of resurrection life.

There are many variants on the resurrection idea and I don't propose to examine them here. But I probably ought to mention that in addition to heaven for the saved, Christians also developed the idea of hell for the damned. Catholic Christians have two further ideas.

For people who have not been baptised into the Christian faith they provide a limbo which is very like the old ideas of Sheol or Hades. And for those Christians who are neither fit for heaven nor hell, they offer purgatory, an afterlife purification period rather like my father's afterlife school. Purgatory is a further preparation to enable people to enjoy heaven.

Nowadays only the more extreme kinds of Christian cling to the idea of damnation and hellfire.

In addition to belief involving reincarnation or resurrection there are spiritualist claims that it is sometimes possible to make contact with those who have died and to have limited converse with them. This is felt to be more likely in the early days after death. Although spiritualism has been attended by a great deal of hocus-pocus, there are some who hold their ideas with great sincerity. There is a similarity between these ideas and the primitive idea that as long as there is flesh on the bones the dead can come back to haunt us.

All of these ideas are based on hope rather than fact. They depend upon faith rather than evidence. For many the hope is winsome and the faith uncertain. For such people the value of their beliefs is slight. They may actually stand in the way of the discovery of the very real comforts we can derive from a purely human approach to bereavement.

But there are some religious people who hold their beliefs with passionate conviction and certainty. They are quite sure that they know the truth. That kind of certitude will obviously bring comfort to them. But when people with that kind of assurance try to impose their views on others, instead of providing comfort they often add to people's distress.

It is important to approach all these different ideas with sensitivity. After all, only a few would be arrogant enough to say categorically that there is no life after death. Without solid evidence we have to say that we do not know one way or the other. But we do emphasise that there is absolutely no solid evidence for any of these beliefs.

Those of us who live our lives without religion are not prepared to hold out a hope that may be false. And we are certainly not prepared to tell people to live their lives on the basis of a hope that may be false.

The absence of solid evidence suggests to us that this life is the only one we have; just as the absence of solid evidence suggests to us that there are no such things or persons as gods. So we live our lives on the assumption that this is the only one.

We do our best to make our lives as fulfilling and as satisfying as we can. Some people feel that this means that we have no comfort to offer to the bereaved. There are certainly some kinds of comfort which we cannot offer. But if those kinds of comfort are only based on hope or faith it is perhaps fair to ask whether

b

anyone else ought to offer them either. We are certainly not prepared to offer a comfort that may turn out to be spurious. We are not prepared to offer an uncertain hope. But we have comfort to offer nevertheless. If I cannot make this clear in the next chapter, I'm quite sure that some of the passages that form the main substance of this book will do so for me.

# V

# Life after Bereavement

When people are overwhelmed by their grief it is hard for them to do anything more than grasp emotional comfort from those who are close to them. The best comfort just then is often to have someone sit with you and hold your hand; or to be held in the arms of someone who loves you.

But once the mind begins to function again, then all kinds of comfort can be found. We seek it within our own human situation. Because we do, it will never be quite the same twice because no two human situations are the same. There is often comfort to be found in the death itself. We speak sometimes of 'a merciful release'. And sometimes we can find comfort where none seems possible. I remember sitting with a young Irish girl, widowed after one month of marriage. Her husband had been a soldier. Early one morning he was driving to his barracks, skidded on black ice, and was killed in the crash. I sat with his widow, holding her hand and feeling absolutely useless. As we sat quietly together she said two things:

'Well at least he never killed anybody else in his life,' and 'I've been his wife. No one can ever take that away from me.'

She was beginning to use her mind to find her own comfort. In the end that is what we all have to do. Sometimes when we want to comfort bereaved people we wonder what we can possibly say that will help. But it is not so much what we say as what we hear that matters. Our primary task is to listen and to act as a sounding board. We enable people to express their grief and to get it out of their system – at least for the moment. We also help them to clutch at the first straws of comfort that come to their minds. If we are listening carefully enough, we can make the most of those straws.

And is that all?

Of course not. But it takes time to discover more lasting comfort. It takes time to get the misery out of our system. And this is where an understanding friend can often be of immense help. Two or three weeks after the funeral the subject of the death in the family suddenly becomes tabu. No one refers to the person who has died because no one wants to open up old sores. And there we are bottling it all up with no one to talk to; no one to share what we are feeling. It is then that we need someone to come to us and make the first move:

'Do you want to talk about it?'

And it all pours out and it is such a relief. And we know that whenever we want to, here is a person who will listen as we talk about our loved one to our heart's content.

It also takes time to discover the comfort of memory. Nowadays adult families are often scattered all over the world so that we see each other rarely. Of course we can write letters. But most of us are bad correspondents. And we can telephone – but most of us have half a thought for the size of our telephone bill. Cheapest of all: we can think about our loved ones. In point of fact we can't avoid it. A thousand and one things will bring them to mind.

Exactly the same is true of those who have died. A thousand and one things bring them to our minds.

If we are part of a family we will often 'see' our loved ones again in gestures, expressions and ways of speaking and acting that have been passed on. And there are so many of the trivial things in life that bring our loved ones back to us vividly. Every time I put my foot on a chair to tie up my shoelace, I can hear my mother ticking my father off for the same crime.

What's more: memory doesn't fade. I was always told that it did. But my own experience is that the more you loved someone, the more their memory stays fresh and vivid. If that can be poignant it can also be joyful – and if you have let your loved one go, the poignancy fades but the joy continues.

All these kinds of comfort involve looking back and dwelling in the past. Is that all there is for us? Is there no life after bereavement? When we have lost our nearest and dearest is there any reason for us to go on living?

At first we may do little more than find comfort for today and a reason for tomorrow. But even that is enough to enable us to go on with life. The rest is partly a matter of time and partly a matter of will and determination.

Earlier in this chapter I mentioned the Irish girl who lost her husband. She was in her twenties when he died. It is obvious that someone in her position can start life again; create a new life; find a new love and build a new joy.

But what about those who are bereaved at the other end of life?

For me, it will always be my father who points the way. My mother died when they were both in their mid-eighties. They had celebrated their diamond wedding a year before she died. For the last few years of her life she had been crippled with arthritis and heavily dependent upon my father. She had been his life. When she died I expected him to follow.

Just how he summed up the will and energy to begin again I don't know. But he did. He began to do all those things he had told us that he wanted to do. I had never believed him. I thought that my mother was his excuse for not doing them. But I was wrong. He built a new life for himself to such purpose that people called him 'the happiest man in Rustington'.

It is true that he had many things going for him – supremely: health and energy. But I am convinced that more than anything else it was his attitude of mind that enabled him to triumph over his grief and begin again so successfully.

I used to visit an elderly woman who was completely housebound. But she retained her interest in her neighbourhood. She knew everything that was going on. When people visited she bombarded them with questions. Because she remained interested she remained interesting and alive. It was always a pleasure to visit her.

When the unbeliever is bereaved, have we nothing to offer? Of course we have.

There are the comforts the mind discovers in the midst of bereavement. There are the comforts provided by the surrounding circle of friends and loved ones. There are the ongoing comforts of joyful and amusing memories. There is the continuing life of our loved one in the lives of the rest of the family – the children and grandchildren – and in the things our loved one has done.

But if our lives are set firmly on this world and this life, we should also be able to turn without any lack of respect or feeling, firmly from the past. Lovingly we leave the past behind and set about the task of creating our own new future, however long or short that may be.

We sit down to dinner with my mother-in-law. When we have finished she is only half way through. How sad it would be if she failed to enjoy the rest of her meal just because we had finished. When our loved ones have completed their feast of life we can learn to go on to enjoy what is left of our own.

Note: My mother-in-law has died since these words were written – not quite as old as my father, she made 91!

# VI

# Where is Comfort to be Found?

At the risk of being repetitive, I have chosen to include the text of a talk I gave at an annual service of remembrance.

There are many people who find comfort in their religious beliefs. And associated with those beliefs there are words of immense comfort in their holy books. But it is not on those things that I wish to focus. Instead I want to focus on all sorts of mundane things which are a part of the everyday experience of all of us.

Oddly enough, comfort is sometimes found in death itself. Sometimes it comes in the way that people die: with courage, without fear, with acceptance, gently, quietly, peacefully. Death isn't always like that but it is often like that.

Thousands of years ago someone wrote: 'O death, how welcome is your sentence to one who is in need and is failing in strength, very old and distracted over everything.'

Death *does* sometimes come as a welcome and merciful relief, both to the person who is dying, and to those whose caring has left them at the end of their tether.

So when death comes peacefully at the end of a long life, death itself can be a comfort. And with it comes the comfort professionals bring when they do their job properly. Sadly, we aren't always happy with the care professionals have given. But when we are, their help is invaluable. I can't number the times I have stood at a funeral and expressed the gratitude of people to those who have gone way beyond the call of duty, whether doctors, nurses, carers in our own homes or in nursing homes, hospitals or the local hospice. At their best, they bring us enormous comfort and help when we most need it.

It is also comforting, of course, when we can look back and know that we ourselves have done our best, sometimes over a long, long period of time. We may not feel that our best was very good. We may wish that we had done more or that we had done things better, been more patient, more understanding and so on. Yet, frail and faulty though we are, we did our best and our loved ones knew that we were doing our best. And since they have died, one or two perceptive people have congratulated us on the care and love we gave. That's a real comfort.

Other comforts come to us as we look back over the lives that have been lived. If someone has had a fairly decent ration of years, we look back over their lives. Those lives were often not easy; there were plenty of hurdles to be overcome; but we see all that our loved ones achieved and accomplished and we see the happiness that marked their best years. They did pretty well, and they did pretty well for us, so there is a kind of completeness about their lives which comforts us.

And of course, as we look back over their lives there are a host of good memories, memories which bring tears and memories which bring laughter and memories which bring both together. Not all memories are comforting but many of them are. And memories bring us two other kinds of comfort.

First there is the awareness of all that death cannot take away. All that we have ever had is ours still. Years of companionship; years of doing things together; hardships and sorrows and triumphs all shared; years of giving and receiving; years of sharing that elusive and wonderful thing called love. All of these things we have had and not even death can take them away from us. Death may bring these things to an end, but it cannot take away what we already have.

And the other comfort memory brings is the recognition that we hold on to *more* than memory. Our loved ones have not just lived alongside us, sharing our lives with us. Something of their very being has entered into us. They have actually become a part of us and it is with lives enriched by them that we shall pursue our onward journey.

32

*      *      *      *

So far I have been talking about ordinary death, death after a decent number of years. But what about the death of the young. But what about all those awful tragedies that some of us have had to face?

When I gave this talk I had in my mind the very first funeral I ever conducted (sixty years before giving this talk). It was the funeral of the baby of a Romany Gypsy family. I had seen her day after day while she was ill and then the family asked me to conduct her funeral. Half a mile of gypsy caravans followed the hearse and there was the kind of profusion of flowers that we saw after the death of Princess Diana.

You would think that nothing could comfort parents when a baby dies, or a youngster just on the cusp of adult life. But the wealth of love with which grieving parents are often surrounded is incredible, absolutely overwhelming, and it is something which lives with you for the rest of your life. We sometimes find that the death of our child enriches us beyond anything we can put into words. The child taken from us can never be forgotten, not just because he or she was our child, but because through that child we have been enriched beyond measure by the love of other people.


As we remember our loved ones, young or old, let us try to remember all that came to us through their dying, all the love and all the kindness.

After many deaths we are rather like surfers riding a wave. We are carried along by the love and friendship of other people – and we are often a bit numb, in a bit of a daze. And we begin to discover that the greatest comfort of all comes from the love and companionship of those who are closest to us: our families and our intimate friends.

And yet there often comes a time when we actually want to be left alone, alone to wander in the garden or to follow an old familiar walk where we can soak up the loveliness of the natural world. Or alone at home faced by that empty chair. We sit in our own old familiar chair with familiar pictures and photographs all around us and the nick-nacks we have picked up on holiday or the gifts given to us on special occasions.

Sometimes we are not quite alone. There is a cat on our lap or the cold nose of a dog who seems to understand, or even one of those very special friends who knows when to be quiet and leave us to ourselves. I remember once visiting an old man whose wife had died.

"Don't offer me sympathy," he said. "It is weakening."

So I didn't offer sympathy. I just sat with him in companionable silence and I think we both felt better for it. For it is in that quietness, that solitude, that something else begins to happen, something that never seems to be mentioned, something which seems to me to be more important than all of the rest – more important even than the love and support given to us by those who are closest to us.

## IT IS THE COMFORT WE FIND
## WITHIN OURSELVES

It lies in our own ability to rise above grief, to take a firm hold on life, and to begin again.

It is amazing what human resources we have if we will only learn to tap into them: resources of courage and grit and determination and will. Death *can* destroy our lives but it *need not* destroy our lives. We *can* begin again. No matter how old we are, we *can* begin again. No matter how devastated we are, we *can* begin again. And there is no tribute we can pay to our loved ones that is better than beginning again.

Even if we didn't know it before we knew them, our shared life with our loved ones taught us how wonderful life can be. The very best way in which we can honour their memory is to learn to live again. Life can never be the same as it was, but it can be wonderful once more. And most of those who have died: *All* of those who loved us for ourselves; would want us to live life to the full again and to find that it is good.

The road ahead is no easy road, but the road behind us has not been easy either. Supported by the love of family and friends and digging deep into our own resources of strength, resilience and character, we can and we must begin to climb out of the valley of the shadow of death into the richness and even into the joy and happiness of the continuing life that beckons to us.

We shall always remember our loved ones. That goes without saying. But we will not allow remembrance to destroy us. We will use our remembrance as a source of inspiration for our lives in the days ahead.

# VII

# What about Anger and Guilt?

Some of the things I have written in this book have already had
an airing in my magazine *The Humanist Theme*. Mrs. Vivien
Gibson wrote to me when my articles appeared and said, 'What
about anger? You have said nothing about anger.'

There must be many things connected with bereavement that I
have left unmentioned – but she was right.

Many people do feel anger when they are faced with death and
many people feel guilt.

Religious people are often so angry with their god for his
injustice that they lose their faith. Others turn to religion in the
hope that it can keep them close to the one who has died.

We are angry because life is so unjust. The young, the healthy,
the 'good' are taken and those who long for death linger on
indefinitely. So we are angry with life or with 'faith'.

We take it out on all sorts of people: doctors, nurses, social
workers, caring relatives. Our anger makes us lash out in all
directions. Often there is no justice in our anger and we know it,
but we are angry just the same. And when we are angry we have
to be angry with someone specific. Professionals are used to
being attacked. That doesn't mean that they are not hurt when
people are unjust, but they do understand. This is not always the
case when we lash out at relatives and friends. We have carried a
heavy load and we feel or say that they have failed to share it. Yet
often, if we are able to be completely honest with ourselves, we

shall find that they wanted to help but we were too possessive to allow them a chance to express their love.

If we could only escape from our preoccupation with ourselves we might discover that they are feeling guilty that they didn't do more. We often do feel that there are things we could have said or done and now it is too late. We regret so many lost opportunities and we feel ashamed that we didn't take more of them.

We are all imperfect. We all miss opportunities. We all have regrets.

But most of us did the best we could. We loved as best we could. Where we failed, our loved one understood and forgave us. After all, our loved one wasn't perfect either – almost, perhaps, but not quite.

Nothing in life is ever quite perfect. So we have to leave behind our past imperfections and get on with making the very best we can of the present and the future. If we have failed the loved one who has died, let us try to love those who are still alive that much more completely. It may be too late to reward those who have died, but if their death contributes to the well-being of the living we shall feel better about them.

Sometimes there are quite specific reasons for our anger or our guilt. When old people die it is usually easy to accept their death because they have had a good innings. It is the death of the young that really gets to us.

We are angry when war or famine, terrorism or disease takes our loved one. We are angry with politicians, terrorists, or a murderer or a driver because they have killed someone before time.

In the last few months I have taken the funerals of two cot death babies; a young man who drowned in his own vomit after an evening's drinking with friends; and two suicides. It could just as easily have been youngsters killed in road accidents or dying from drugs, aids or other illnesses.

Deaths of young people often make us angry at the sheer injustice of life. But they can affect us in much more personal ways. We may feel that we have in some way caused the death, or at very least failed to prevent it. So we are filled with remorse and are angry with ourselves and our closest companions. Or we may be angry with the person who has died. How dare he leave us? He had no right to go, leaving so many problems and burdens behind. He could still have been with us if only he had behaved differently. Or we are angry with his friends. And sometimes we feel guilty ourselves as if we drove him to his death.

It is perhaps this anger with ourselves and its associated feelings of guilt that is the hardest to bear. Why did we not do more, love better, express our devotion while we had the chance.

So many of us feel anger in the presence of death that it is clear that anger is a natural reaction to death.

I can't stress that enough: Anger is a natural reaction to death.

If we can recognise and accept that fact, we are half way to dealing with our own anger.

Anger needs to be both recognised and expressed. If we don't express it, it can easily turn into bitterness. Bitterness is no good to anyone. But if we express our anger we can get it out of our system and allow our minds to take over and make what sense they can of things.

Sometimes there isn't a lot of sense to be made. Life is often unjust and cruel. We have to learn to face that fact and to accept it with resignation. It has to be accepted, not because we approve of it, but because we can do nothing to alter it.

Where that is not the case; where we can do things to alter the injustice of life; grief and its attendant anger can often be the starting point of devoted work to improve the human lot. We all know of people who have suffered a death in the family (let us say from cancer or heart disease). Some of them go on to devote their time and resources to research into the causes and cure of that particular illness.

Under such circumstances our anger can lead to great benefit for other people and to the feeling that perhaps the suffering and death of our loved one were not altogether in vain.

So: if you feel angry, let your anger out. If it is possible feed it into appropriate channels that will turn it into something positive and good. And if that is not possible, at least get it out of your system and let your reason take over. Facing the death of a loved one is never easy. In the end the only real way to face it is to leave it behind. Our loved one has gone and we are left. Without disrespect, we must say our farewells and turn back to life. Time is short.

How short, none of us can know. Any loved one worth his salt will want his survivors to enjoy life to the full. The best way to cope with death is to turn back to life and live with all our power.

# Postscript

I find that I have said very little about long term debilitating illnesses or about dementia. These are often the illnesses that make us most angry. And it is often our inability to cope with such illnesses that gives us much grief and leads us into feelings of guilt. Again and again I find myself faced with people who have done their utmost over a long period and their only reward is devastating internal turmoil and complete exhaustion.

There is no *quick* fix.

We need understanding, patient, loving friends or family. We need people who are equally ready to be with us or to stand back and allow us space. We probably need medical pick me ups and sleeping aids for a while. We need the chance to recover our strength and to build up our inner resources again – to recuperate.

When we have reached the bottom of the pit there is no further down that we can go. Then, if we search hard enough, we shall find that there are steps leading up out of the pit. And there are people above us who are holding out their hands to help us up.

Recovery and renewal *are* possible. New life *is* possible.

# VIII
# Grief

Sometimes there is a bleak emptiness and desolation in grief.
Tennyson captures it in one of his poems:

> 'Break, break, break,
> On thy cold gray stones, O sea!
> And I would that my tongue could utter
> The thoughts that arise in me.
>
> O well for the fisherman's boy,
> That he shouts with his sister at play!
> O well for the sailor lad,
> That he sings in his boat on the bay!
>
> And the stately ships go on
> To their haven under the hill;
> But O for the touch of a vanished hand
> And the sound of a voice that is still!
>
> Break, break, break,
> At the foot of thy crags, O Sea!
> But the tender grace of a day that is dead
> Will never come back to me.'

We have to find our own way past that and no one can do it for
us. But when grief fills our whole being and seems so completely

overwhelming and destructive we can see no way forward. Nor are we sure that we actually *want* to go forward and when people tell us that we must, we feel that they are being insensitive and cruel.

Yet these people are right. We can either go down Queen Victoria road and become the despair of our friends, self-pitying, self-destructive, withering and shrinking towards our own demise, or we can learn to grow and to live again.

No sensible person will ask us to deny our grief. What our friends will ask of us is that we *grow*, so that, instead of being all-embracing and all-encompassing, our grief becomes part of a larger whole.

People say all sorts of things about grief. They say that 'time heals' but that is not necessarily true. All that time does is to give us opportunities which we can take or reject. It gives us the opportunity to escape from the overwhelming nature of grief into something calmer, quieter and more positive just as a rushing river comes crashing into the quietness and stillness of a lake.

People also say that grief grows less with the years. Certainly the *pain* of grief may grow less. But if people are implying that we forget, then they are wrong. Where there has been real love and real loss, we never forget. Nor do we want to. On the contrary, we want to remember and to cherish what we have had. We want to carry our loved one with us into the future. But we have to learn to do that without allowing our grief to destroy our lives or to harm the lives of other people who love us. And sometimes that is not easy.

Have you ever tried to put something into a box only to find that it won't quite go? We try this way and that but it doesn't matter how many ways we try, it just won't fit. In the end we either break the box or behave more sensibly and go and find a larger box.

Our lives are within a box. For a while the box is so full of grief that there is no room for anything else. We have no intention of throwing the grief away. It is our connection with the life that has gone. What we need is a bigger box with room for our grief and also with room for all those new elements which can make the future bearable, possible, positive, even happy. So we have to grow the box – put in extra panels all round so that it becomes big enough to contain everything valuable from the past and everything we want to add in the future.

If we are really to work our way through our grief and come out of it the other side we have to learn how to be bigger, better and more complete people. That way we can take our loved ones with us and keep them safe in our hearts for the rest of our days but we can also start again and move on.

# IX
# Returning to Joy

There are many different kinds of bereavement. All of them leave scars and all of them impose some kind of loneliness on us. For most of us the worst loneliness of all follows the death of a partner.

In countries like ours there are multitudes of lonely widows and widowers, all of them feeling that their experience is unique. There are times when all of us long for solitude but enforced solitude is a different matter altogether. Every little job becomes a burden. All the things we have always done and take in our stride suddenly seem mountainous. We long for someone to share the trivia of everyday life; for the companionship of an armchair filled.

Overcoming such loneliness is never easy. But it can be achieved. The very first thing we have to do is to learn not to be sorry for ourselves. Nothing loses friends so quickly.

Curiously enough, it is as we bully ourselves into doing those jobs we have been dreading that we begin to find the solace of an occupied body and mind. Whether we like it or not, life has to go on. As we begin to tackle the ordinary tasks of everyday life we find that our own death wish begins to fade. The normal human desire for life reasserts itself. It is time now to find and to focus on the joys of solitude.

As we have seen, memory is one of them. But memory is not unmitigated joy. Particularly in the early days it can bring as

43

much desolation as comfort. It is only after what someone has called 'the healing years' that memory is all comfort.

Another of the joys of solitude is the rediscovery of ourselves. For years we have lived for someone else. Our lives have been governed at least in part, by our partner's wishes, our partner's way of life, pleasures, sensitivities, needs. Now we have only ourselves to consider. How do we want to spend our time? What do we want to do with ourselves and our lives?

There are new freedoms and new anxieties. I read once of a widow who had to conquer her fear of driving long distances alone. Most widows would first have to conquer the much more mundane fear of filling their own car with petrol. And widowers have to learn to cook, to clean and to shop.

In a way, it is going through a process of growing up all over again. We grow up into the new life that is ours. Every day we seem to face something new. But each day also brings a sense of accomplishment in what we have achieved. We begin to make all sorts of discoveries about ourselves and the vast untapped resources we possess.

Oddly enough, the supreme joy of solitude is the joy of companionship. Some areas of life close to us when we lose our partners. There are functions where everybody else is paired off and we feel out of place. But it often works the other way.

Precisely because we are alone, we are free to make new friends. We are freer to meet strangers, freer to talk and to listen. We no longer have to look over our shoulder wondering what our loved one would think of our friendship or our behaviour. We can respond freely and openly to every approach others make.

Solitude is often spoken about as a time of peace and tranquillity. Sometimes it may be. More often it is a time when our thoughts and feelings run riot and have to be brought under control. Someone called solitude 'a threshing floor of emotions'.

Provided we can separate grain and chaff we can turn our solitude into the secure base from which we venture out into our continuing journey through life. It is no insult to the memory of our loved ones to acknowledge that part of that adventure is only possible because they have gone. We travelled joyfully with them in the past. Now we are on a solo voyage which can also prove to be a lot of fun.

So smile through the tears, and when the tears are done smile on. There are joys still to come for those who will look for them and create them.

# Part Two:

## *Comforting Words*

# Comforting Words

The second part of this book contains pieces I have written myself and a few that I have reshaped from the writings of others (enough to make them my own). Many of them have been a response to a particular death and some have been a response to griefs of my own.

In earlier editions of *Coping with Death* I included a good deal of work by other people. But there is so much available now in book form or on the internet (although not always accurate or attributed to the right author) that I have decided only to include my own work or work in which I have shared in this volume. But, as will become clear, my own work has often been sparked by the work or words of others.

# Going to a funeral

Going to a funeral is a bit like going
to a railway station to say goodbye to
someone we love. As the train moves
slowly away from us we wave goodbye and
watch them out of sight until the last
trace of the train is gone.

Sometimes, of course, we are reasonably
cheerful because we know that it will
not be long before we stand waiting for
their train to arrive.

But as we grow older we are less sure.
Will this be the final farewell? Their
train moves away and we feel that we may
never enjoy another arrival. We leave
the station with sadness in our hearts
as we turn back to the continuation of
our own lives.

So it is with death. We see the departure
and know that there is no return. But after
a while we begin to realise that we can
never lose those things we already have.
We can never lose the experiences of love
that we have shared nor can we ever lose
the rich fund of memories that our shared
lives have given to us.

*While reading Tennyson's **Idylls of the King***

I would not be holy
as the hermit or the monk.

No. I would come to death
from the heart of the world's life
bearing the scars of many battles.

And some will be the scars of victory,
and some, borne sad but openly,
the marks of my defeat.

The good fight I would fight,
though fight and often lose,
and thus would come through life.

Let me but reach my end
open and honest
and without hypocrisy.


## Death

When I was a boy
I sometimes went to bed
by candlelight.

The last task
was to blow out the candle
or snuff it out
between finger and thumb.

Death is no more than that –
a negative,
it is not man's enemy.

In simple truth
it is precisely that,
nothing at all,
just the snuffing out of life's flame.

# ... to Quietness and Sleep

In the night of weariness
I will not force my flagging spirit
nor drive my overburdened mind,
nor yet persist
with pointless fears
or vain imaginings.

Night draws its veil
over the tired eyes of the day.
I leave behind the confusion,
the noise and clamour of my life's concerns
and give myself up
to quietness and sleep.

Perhaps to sleep for ever,
but whether for me or for you
the darkness will vanish
and the morning will surely come
to renew the sight with dawn
in a fresh gladness of awakening.

*(This owes much to the poems of Rabindranath Tagore.)*

# Life's Pool

We are like children
with hands full of stones
standing beside a pool of still water.

One by one we cast the stones
filling the pool with ripples
counteracting one another
or blending with one another.

But the ripples die away.

The pool returns to stillness
when the last stone
has been thrown.

49

c

# On the Death of a Child

and when she died
we mourned our loss
and cried in anger
and in pain.

we soldiered on
took strength from friends
who wrapped us round
and took the strain.

between ourselves we shared our love
and shared our pain,
we found our way
to life again.

we're stronger now
live deeper lives,
and all because
she came and died.


# Death

The struggle of life is ended
in silence and in sleep.

Oblivion comes
and rest from pain
and peace from care.

No more the haunted soul,
no more the tortured mind,
no more the fevered brow.

Oblivion comes
and rest from pain
and peace from care.

# A hymn: Life's Full Circle

Life has many things to offer,
love brings joy beyond compare;
not in solitude we find them,
family and friends all share.

Excellence is what we strive for,
wholeness is the human goal.
So we seek our own fulfilment
in a caring, sharing role.

Eagerly we grasp life's riches,
eagerly we set them free,
prodigal with what life gives us,
glad a source of joy to be.

And in times of pain and crisis
or in sorrow's lonely hour
we bring home the strength and solace
of our love's renewing power.

Swift our lives run their full circle
'from the cradle to the grave',
so we live each day's adventure
to the full, and nothing save.

Then, when falls life's final curtain,
peacefully we take our rest
leaving those who love and mourn us
knowing that we lived our best.


This may be sung to the tune specially written for it:
*Life's Full Circle* by Brendon Renwick, or to the hymn tune:
*Love Divine* by J. Stainer 1840-1901.

# Death Wishes

Dear medics,
        there's no need to strive
so hard to keep this chap alive.

I've had far more of weal than woe
and if it's now my time to go
I'm pretty nearly umpty five
and unconcerned if death arrive.

Use all the bits of me you can
to help some other maid or man.

Those who survive me will agree
tis better to go with dignity
than cling to some poor hollow sham
an ancient relic of a man.

If I were conscious or au fait
I'd end things now and not delay.

I've no religion and no god
so, even if you think it's odd,
I pray you let me go in peace –
as far as may be from a priest.

# Grief

Death may be nothing
but grief is hell.
The agony of loss
and no one to tell.

The plans destroyed,
the emptiness of life;
the things unsaid
to husband or wife.

'Ashes to ashes and
dust back to dust',
and the long slow journey
back to life if I must.

# Life's Joys

Thankful am I that I have lived in this great world
And known its many joys:

the thrill of mountains
and the morning air,
hills and the lonely heather covered moors,
harvest and the strong sweet scent of hay;

a rock-strewn river overhung with trees,
shafts of sunlight in a valley leading to the sea,
the beat of waves on rough and rocky shores
and wild, white spray flung high in ecstasy:

the song of birds awakening at dawn
and flaming sunsets at the close of day
with cooling breezes in the secret night –
music at night and moonlight on the sea;

the comfort of my home and treasured things,
the love of kin and fellowship of friends,
firelight and laughter and children at their play
with all their hopes and dreams,
their freshness as the future beckons them;

the faithful eyes of dogs, companionship of cats,
my garden with its rich reward for toil,
and all those things that make life dear and beautiful.

The tapestry of life, both joy and pain
is ours to live but once and not again.
When I look back upon my richly varied years,
I crave no more.
Thankful am I that I have lived
So shed no tears.

*(This began as a prayer by Elizabeth Craven. I have re-written
it so many times that I have no idea how much of the original
remains and must apologise to the author.)*

# A Grave

It's good to have a place to go,
a place of pilgrimage you know,
a place to pause, remember, think and stare,
a place to feel that he is there.

It's good to have a place to go
where we can say, 'we miss you so'.
In this calm spot we are at ease
knowing that you have found your peace.

We know we must begin again
and find new ways to ease our pain
but there will always be a space
within our hearts – your own dear place.

And sometimes as we slip away
we'll almost seem to hear you say,
'Thanks for the past. It meant so much.
Through heart and mind you'll keep in touch.'

# Nothing from the Past has Gone

When someone dies,
someone from our family
or a close and well-loved friend,
somehow we feel
that we are less than once we were.

Reduced in stature,
something in ourselves has died,
something of our life has gone,
irretrievably gone
and lost for ever.

Slowly, so slowly, we discover deeper truths.
Nothing has gone save only the present and future presence,
the warm companionship
that has meant so much.

All that we have ever known remains:
all the memories we have treasured,
all the fun and all the laughter,
all the love and all the friendship:
nothing from the past has gone.

*(After reading John Donne's famous poem.)*

## 'Ad gloriam per spinas'

Life is not always kind or good.
Sometimes it seems
that fate has dealt
a rotten hand.

Each rising tide
is followed by the ebb.
Each minor victory
is beaten down.

And yet folk battle on,
grim-faced, determined,
forcing themselves
to find their own way through.

And here and there
along the way
a moment's triumph
brings them joy.

Friendship supports
and strengthens them
and love brings light
into the darkest hour.

Through all the thorns
they've struggled on
'til watchers praise
all they have done.

*A friend gave me some words of Rabindranath Tagore. They had already been adapted and didn't altogether make sense (to me). So I've adapted them again!*

## Farewell my Friends

It was beautiful
as long as it lasted,
the journey of my life.
I have no regrets
whatsoever, save
the pain I leave behind,
those dear hearts
who love and care . . .

At every turning of my life
I came across good friends,
friends who stood by me,
whose strong arms held me up
when my strength let me down.

Farewell, farewell my friends.
I smile and bid you goodbye.
No. Shed no tears
for I need them not.
All I need is your smile.

## 'To live in the hearts of those we love is not to die.'

We none of us look forward to the actual business of dying but when it is over we slip into 'the care-free calm of death' knowing that life itself goes on and that something of our own life continues in the people we have loved and the things we have done. 'To live in the hearts of those we love is not to die.'

57

## Pooh Sticks

They were playing Pooh sticks,
dropping them into the river
on one side of the bridge
and running to see
whose would pass beneath it first.

Their father watched a stick
carried by the current
of the stream
until it was out of sight.

'That's it,' he thought.
'We are dropped into the stream of life
and carried by the current,
who knows where.

Will our journey be cut short,
ending in a pile of driftwood
by the river bank,
or will we find our way,
twisting and turning, bumped and bruised,
until we end up lost in the sea?'

# A Clockwork Toy

Sometimes it seems as though life is
rather like an old clockwork toy.

Fully wound it rushes through the early
years. But as the spring unwinds it
begins to slow until at last it comes
to a full stop. Its noise and movement
fall silent.

Childlike, we turn away and play with
other of our toys. But that is as it
should be. The best tribute we can
pay to those who have died is to

turn from death to life again and to
live our own lives positively and well.

# The Question

The question is not
how far did you go
but what did you see and do
as you travelled on your journey.

# Time

Time is not measured by the ticking of a clock
nor by the passing of the hours and days.
Time is measured in moments that are memorable,
in experiences that are precious to us.

So let us make the most of all our days,
living them out in warmth of friendship
and in depth of love –
spending each precious moment 'as if it were our last'.

*Faced with the death of a young drug addict I sat with a family who found it desperately hard to find ANYTHING positive to say. But slowly, as we talked, a few precious memories began to emerge. When I got home I found myself writing:*

## Remember the Good Times

Remember the GOOD times,
remember only those.

There were good times you know,
smart times, cheerful times,
happy times when I was young
and life was good
and all the family was there.

Remember the good times,
remember only those.

Times of work and times of friendship,
times of love and times of courtship,
times of fun and times of laughter,
there were good times you know.

So forget the rest.
Just remember the good times,
remember only those.

## When I am Gone

When I am gone,
release me, let me go,
You mustn't tie yourself to me in tears.
Be happy that we had so many years.

I gave to you my love,
You can only guess
how much you gave to me
in happiness.

Grieve awhile for me
if grieve you must,
then let your grief be comforted.
I trust

you'll bless the memories
that I have sown
and I thank you
for the love you each have shown.

*(I have revised this anonymous piece.)*

# In the midst of life we are in death

Life comes and goes.
The existence of man fluctuates,
tragic situations bring out the best in people,
love and understanding bind the broken-hearted.

The death of a friend so young
makes us reject
the averages of life,
and some of the world's values.

Life may be long
or short.
We must make the most of what we have,
live life to the full.

And we must come to terms with death,
not grieve excessively.
Time cannot cure the intense heartache
but may ease the pain.

**Christine Scrase**

*(One of her early poems which I have adapted slightly.)*

# The Death of a Child

There were so many hopes and dreams
there was so much joy
and now there is so much sorrow
and all our words seem empty and to no avail.

We wanted her so much
and what we thought was a promise for the future
has been taken from us
leaving us empty and numb and lost.

Yet even now,
perhaps most of all, now,
the arms of love enfold us
and hold us within their care.

In our own times of greatest weakness
the strength of those we love
is there for us to feed upon
and so to recover our own strength and life.

Little by little we take up the threads
and begin our lives again,
taking all the joy and sorrow with us
and building it all into a greater whole.

# No One Saw it Coming

No one saw it coming.
He seemed
like any other healthy, happy lad.
Twenty years old,
he hanged himself.

The family blame themselves
but no one is to blame
except perhaps the man himself.
Twenty years old,
he hanged himself:

They had invested
so much love
in this child of theirs.
Twenty years old,
he hanged himself.

Shocked, numb and anguished,
he leaves such pain,
but grief and pain are all in vain.
Twenty years old,
he hanged himself.

Without the child they loved so well
they have to try
to live again.
Twenty years old,
he hanged himself.

# Ripe for the Harvest

When the apples are green
they can only be picked by force,
ripped from the tree unwillingly.

So it is with the death of the young,
it comes so often with violence
and tears them from our lives.

But when apples have ripened to maturity,
they fall from the tree by themselves
or are picked with ease.

So it is with the death of the old.
Death comes when the time is ripe
and when we ourselves are 'ripe for the harvest'.

*From an idea taken from Cicero.*
*The phrase quoted is from something I read*
*as a young man – from Leslie Church?)*

'I think I am in this body –
I really only think it.'
                    Jorie Graham

------------------------------------------------------------

It's a peculiar sensation.
Thoughts really are
independent of our bodies.
They take wings.

Do any other creatures
have thoughts
or is it our thoughts
that make us human?

I sit here
but in my thoughts
I can be with my sons
or with my daughters.

I can be wherever I wish
with whoever I wish.
We speak of 'calling them to mind' –
A simple thought and they are there

with us, standing beside us,
the living and the dead.
It makes no difference:
a simple thought and they are there.

My body is the home
of my mind
but my mind
is as free as the wind.

# Too Late

I learned too late that you were gone.
We had no chance to say goodbye.
I grieve far more than I can say.
I miss you every single day.

There is so much I wanted to tell you,
so much that I wanted to say
but now you've been taken away from us,
yes now, you are too far away.

Does it matter that I never told you
the things that I wanted to say?
Did you know all those things never spoken
before you were taken away?

Yes, yes, deep down I know you knew.
You knew the way that I loved you.
We did not need the words unsaid
for love lies deep in heart and head.

*(This is a revised version of my earlier
    poem of the same title.)*

# Not with Tears

So many people,
all of them important to our lives
have gone:
all gone and what is the nature of our grief?

Life is so precious and so full.
Even when it seems insignificant,
dull, empty, meaningless,
it is still too rich to waste on idle tears.
There is no point in looking back
or wasting time on might-have-beens.

Life is for living, not for mourning.
They lived. They left their mark. They died.
I live, and while I live, I'll live
and if and when I think of them,
I'll think with gratitude of all they gave
and of all they were.

Now that we're older and life is less demanding
we have more time to think of them
and we do think of them, but not with tears,
nor with an outpouring of useless grief.
We think with thankfulness that they have been a part,
such a significant part of our lives.

And one day soon, we shall be gone
and some will think of us
but not, we hope, with tears.
We've been together many years,
we've lived, we've made our little mark.
It won't matter much to add,
'They've died.'

## A Greek-style epigram

Do not raise a rich and useless
monument after I am gone.
When I am dead what will it matter to
me whether people know who I was or
not. Throw my ashes to the wind
or let them fertilise a tree.

## A snippet

Creative men and women leave visible
reminders of their lives for us to cherish
and enjoy,
Loving men and women leave their
imprint on our lives, and these we
cherish most of all.

# Grief

*(Most of the words of this come from a poem by Shelley,
but they have been completely re-ordered and re-shaped
into this expression of grief:)*

Leave me not old and drear and comfortless.
Stay yet awhile. Speak to me once again.
Alas, that all I loved of her should be
as if it had not been. . .
She will awake no more, oh never more.
She is made one with nature.

That light whose smile kindled my universe,
that beauty in which all my life has worked and moved
is passed from the revolving year.
She has departed. I should now depart.
No more let life divide
what death can join together.

# Dementia

*'Many of us will one day lose ourselves,*
*our place in the world' and*
*'who will we be then?' – Philip Cross*

When we no longer know
the people we have loved
yet find a quiet peace,
content in emptiness,

no troubles trouble us,
no strife, no stress, no strain,
no debts, no doubts, nor anything
to burden us with pain.

Safe in a lost cocoon
awaiting nought but death,
oblivious to all else,
we are free from every fear.

Our anguished loved ones
see us move beyond recall
and cling to shreds – a smile,
some hint you know just who we are.

But who we are and who you are,
who knows? For those who watch and care
there's nought but grief,
the grief of loss and death in life.

At last death comes, oh friendly death
who comes so gently in the end,
softly 'with healing in his wings'
and leaves us free for other things.

## An Old Man's Death

When someone old has reached his end
there is no call to weep or wail.
The lives of those who live
need not be spoiled by grief.

When our work is done,
our bodies old and frail,
we can accept without regret
the fact our time has come.

The fire of life dies down,
the embers spit and spark
and then fade out, burnt out,
and so the fire is gone.

The thread of life is cut
which often brings relief.
When peace has come why spoil it all
with overwhelming grief?

For somewhere close at hand
another fire is burning.
New life is here, young, full and warming:
its time has come to burn and blaze and shine.

## For Tom, who built and flew model airplanes

Wind buffeted, the plane
was soaring in the yellow light.
Reaching for the heavenly height
it soared away in lonely flight.

It was very nearly lost to sight
when it broke free from his control.
He felt such loss. This was never right,
but a broken plane can be made whole.

When those we love are lost to sight
we sometimes feel it isn't right
and always feel appalling loss.
A broken heart can't be made whole.

And yet, that image of pure flight
which takes us up beyond the clouds
paints pictures that are full of peace.
He is in peace. That much is right.

*This poem owes a little to a poem of Charlie Garnell, one of a number shown to me by his widow many years ago.*

73

d

*'I knew if you had died that I should grieve*
*Yet I found my heart wishing you were dead.'*
*Samuel Beckett*


There are so many of us
who think the thought
and feel the guilt of it
yet never speak the words out loud.

But if we do,
people are shocked,
people less close who hear the words
and fail to see the grief.

There are so many times
when loved ones live too long,
too long for their heart's ease,
too long for ours.

Nor is it only those grown old,
grown weak, in pain,
with nothing in their lives to make
them wish to wake from sleep again.

Even some young,
some sick or injured young
live lives without a shred of hope
that life can give them joy again.

I too have found my aching heart
wishing some loved one could find death
and peace at last, no matter that
my guilt and grief would still go on.

# Too Long

Death rarely gets his timing right.
Sometimes we live too long
and those who love us best
wish we were dead.

They cannot speak of it of course,
not now, not later
when at last we've gone.
It would not do to say that we are glad.

Sometimes we live too long
and are the first to recognise
and speak of it.
People protest.

'Methinks that they protest too much.'
And then perhaps we make that awful plea.
We have not made a move to kill ourselves
so now we ask for what is not allowed.

Humans must suffer on and on,
only their pets can be set free,
but now we lay the burden of it all
on those who love us best
and wish that we were dead.
Death rarely gets his timing right.

And shall I tell the truth my friend?
Shall I, this once, the guilty truth reveal?
There have been those I loved
who lived too long
and yes, sometimes,
I wished that they were dead.

I feel no guilt for feeling so.
In life I loved them
and I love them still.
There can come times when love,
yes, kindest, truest love,
can wish a loved one dead.

# Closure

Closure – as if we can put a life
in a box, lay it on a shelf
or stuff it in a kitchen drawer
and forget about it for ever.

There is no closure
while one of us remains alive
with our unanswered questions,
those questions we could never –
never thought – to ask.

This is the nature of haunting:
the things we want to know
and now will never know
because the answers
are the things that died.

But then we wonder
how much it matters anyway.
He – she – has left so many memories
and most of them are good.

And this is also the nature of haunting
the pleasure of remembering,
the warmth of recollection,
the joy that once they lived
and shared our lives.

# An Elderly 'If'

If we have had a reasonable ration of years,
if we have made some contribution to the lives of others
if we have mostly done our best
and lived our lives both positively and well,
if we have loved and if we have been loved
and if we leave a family we can call our own
we shall not fear when life comes to its end
nor even mind too much.

'Hand clasps hand across the years
and we are one' and now our children
and their children will travel on.

*The quote is from Eric Ambler.*

*Although the words of these two poems are the words of Rabindranath Tagore, I have taken them from different places and re-worked them just enough to make them my own.*

## Taking Leave

*(from Rabindranath Tagore)*

I have got my leave.
Bid me farewell my friends.
I bow to you all and take my departure.
Here I give back the keys of my door
and I give up all claims to my house.

I only ask for last kind words from you.
We were neighbours for long,
but I received more than I could give.
Now the day has dawned
and the lamp that lit my dark corner is out.

When I go from hence
let this be my parting word,
that what I have seen is unsurpassable.
At this time of my parting
the sky is flushed with dawn.

I have no fear in my mind.

# Life and Death

*(from Rabindranath Tagore)*

It was my part at the feast of life
to play upon my instrument,
and I have done all I could.

In life, I found that
when old words die out on the tongue,
new melodies break forth from the heart;

I found that
when the path before me was closed
and the old tracks were lost,
new country was revealed
with all its wonders.

But now
I have come to the last limit of my power
and my provisions are exhausted.
It is time to take shelter
in a silent obscurity,
knowing that death, my death,
is the last fulfilment of my life.

# Farewell

The final path we all must take
oft comes to us too soon
and we'd like to go another way
but we're crying for the moon.

For some that dreaded pathway
seems a never ending road,
and they long to reach their final goal
and greet it like a friend.

If this is my end, then let me go.
As I slip from your lives have no regrets.
My life is done and yours go on –
yours are the lives that matter now.

I do not ask 'remember me'.
I only want what's best for you.
Make the most of life and have some fun,
enjoy each other 'til life is done.

We've had our moments, you and I,
and made each other laugh and cry.
And faced with life's great question marks
we've never bothered to ask why.

If at some moment when life's bad
you think of me, then don't be sad.
Just think of how I made you mad,
kick up your heels, laugh and be glad.

For soon or late, the journey's done,
we've travelled life away
and mixed within the sheer hard graft
we've found some time to play.

And that's what life is all about,
a bit of work, a bit of play,
enjoying friendship, even love
until we can no longer stay.

# Waiting for Something to Happen

*(The quotation is from a poem by Andrew Motion.)*

The old horse stood there
'waiting for something important to happen,
only nothing ever did,
beyond the next day and the next,
and the one leading to another.'

And when you no longer have to go to work
no longer have anything in particular
that you have to do,
nothing in particular to get up for,
there is a real danger
that old age may become just like that,
waiting for something, anything to happen,
and knowing that ultimately
there is just one thing that will happen.

# After a Death

*(The quotation is from a poem by Betty Shipway.)*

'Some small part of me has also died
looking at his vacant chair.'

And yet so much of me remains alive
and there's so much of life in which to thrive.
So much of life every day we live alone
doing the things we have to do;
doing the things we love to do;
and he was never part of those.

Only when the doing's done and we sit down
do we have time to think of him.
A memory, a photograph
will bring him back; create a laugh;
and strangely, though he's gone, he's there,
but not the burden of his care.

# Life's Journey

I'm travelling on a journey
and the end is drawing near.
The engine's running out of steam
with creaks and screaming joints
I'm slowing down.

It's been a lengthy journey
so I've been a lucky man,
and mostly I've enjoyed it,
travelling without a plan.

Things happened in my early years
and time just raced me by.
Things happened and I never thought
to ask the reason why.

If the journey's been a good one
and as long as mine has been
with lots of pleasure on the route
and lots that you have seen
the journey's end is welcome
sometimes can't arrive too soon.

Life's secret is the journey
and the stops along the way,
the people travelling with you,
companions night and day.

Life's not a pilgrimage.
There is no heaven and no hell.
The destination's meaningless,
just a station marked 'The End',
but if the journey's been a good one
that station is a welcome friend.

Yes, journey's end is meaningless:
just the squealing of the brakes
and then a final gentle jolt

## 'Nothing we can see.'

*(from Andrew Motion's poem in memory
of Elizabeth Dalley.)*

(We) watched, and saw the air
you left for us to breathe
grow solid, then like water
close above your head,
and your life slip out of reach. . .

in time the world
wears down to simple rock,
then boulders, pebbles, stones,
then grains of shrinking sand,
then nothing we can see.

'Nothing we can SEE'
but so much we can feel,
remember and appreciate;
so much we carry forward,
an ingrained part of us
and of our innermost being.

'Nothing we can see'
but so very much
we cannot fail to be.

*(These last two verses are my own.)*

# At a Graveside

*(Revised from a poem by J.L. Crommelin Brown.*

Above the seasons haste away,
and skies are fair in spring,
but all the seasons are one with you,
summer and winter have done with you,
and autumn's leaves have gone astray.

Surely this is a goodly gift
to sleep so sound and sure
that neither grief nor weariness,
passion, nor pain, nor dreariness
can touch you anymore.

## The Graveside

I stood alone beside the grave
beneath a blue and cloud-strewn sky
and set aside the question 'why?',
seeking instead to let the day
gentle my heart and dry my eye.

A thousand memories flooded in
and each was special in its way.
On that quiet, warmth-filled sunny day,
standing in that light so clear
I felt that s/he was very near.

Our past was very close to me
but then a burst of blackbird's song
told me I must be moving on
holding those memories of the past
but living fully while I last.

*(Sparked by a poem by Brian O'Boyle.)*

# Nothing from the Past has Gone

When someone dies
someone from our family
or a close and well-loved friend,
somehow we feel
that we are less than once we were.

Reduced in stature,
something in ourselves has died,
something of our life has gone,
irretrievably gone
and lost for ever.

Slowly, so slowly, we discover deeper truths.
Nothing has gone
save only the present and future presence,
the warm companionship
that has meant so much.

All that we have ever known remains:
all the memories we have treasured,
all the fun and all the laughter,
all the love and all the friendship:
nothing from the past has gone.

# Prayers and Blessings:

A religious ceremony will always contain prayers. A non-religious ceremony will often contain a period of silence 'for personal reflection and for those who wish to, to say their prayers.' That is absolutely right. *We should always seek to be as inclusive as possible.* But sometimes I am asked to go further than that – to lead prayers. Can it be done with a good conscience? Have a look at this which is introduced as 'a period of guided reflection or prayer':

> Let us honour those who live quietly and gently on the earth, charming the lives of others with the warmth of their kindness and the depth of their friendship.
>
> Using words of Paul in the New Testament, let us give thanks for a life shared and enjoyed: 'Whatever has been true, whatever honourable, whatever has been just, whatever pure, whatever has been lovely, whatever gracious; whatever there has been of excellence, anything worthy of praise', let us give thanks for these things.
>
> And may those who mourn find comfort, strength and support in the days ahead and a new strength of purpose to drive their own lives forward.

Here is something similar which is derived from a Christian book of services but adapted for universal use:

> In sorrow may we find consolation, support and strength; may we be grateful for all those good things we have been given; and may we draw closer to one another in friendship and in love.
>
> May each one of us become the strength of the weak, the comfort of the sorrowful, the friend of the lonely, and in so doing may we find and establish our own peace.

# So much for prayer, what about blessings?

A religious ceremony will often end with a blessing and there are some very beautiful blessings in the Bible and in religious liturgies. These are often immensely comforting and reassuring.

A non-religious ceremony will not bless anybody in the name of a god, but it can end in positive hopes and good wishes, and sometimes religious blessings can be adapted. Here is an adaptation of words of Cardinal Newman:

> May human love and friendship support us all the day long until the shades lengthen and the evening comes; until the busy world is hushed, the fever of life is over and our work is done. Then may our lives move gently to their appointed end, blessed by safe lodging, rest and peace.

Among the poems there are expressions similar to this, which is Celtic:

> The peace of the running water to you,
> the peace of the flowing air to you,
> the peace of the quiet earth to you,
> the peace of the shining stars to you,
> and the love and the care of us all to you.

It is good to end a ceremony on a note of hope, good wishes and peace and I felt that it might be good to end this book in the same way so I'll finish with some closing words of my own:

> In days to come
>
> if we are troubled
> may we find peace;
>
> if we are depressed,
> may we find joy;
>
> and if we are lonely,
> may we find companionship and love.